Cloudy with a Fire in the Basement

*Cloudy with a Fire
in the Basement*

RONNA BLOOM

PEDLAR PRESS | Toronto

COPYRIGHT © 2012 Ronna Bloom

ALL RIGHTS RESERVED. No part of this book may be
reproduced or transmitted in any form or by any means
whatsoever without written permission from the publisher,
except by a reviewer, who may quote brief passages in a review.
For information, write Pedlar Press at PO Box 26, Station P,
Toronto Ontario M5S 2S6 Canada.

ACKNOWLEDGEMENTS
The publisher wishes to thank the Canada Council for the Arts
and the Ontario Arts Council for their generous support of our
publishing program.

LIBRARY AND ARCHIVES CANADA
CATALOGUING IN PUBLICATION

Bloom, Ronna, 1961-
        Cloudy with a fire in the basement / Ronna Bloom.

Poems.
ISBN 978-1-897141-51-9

    I. Title.

PS8553.L665C56 2012   C811'.54   C2012-903730-3

COVER ART   Susan Warner Keene, *Leaf No. 1*, 2012

DESIGN   Zab Design & Typography, Toronto

TYPEFACE   Adobe Garamond

Printed in Canada

CONTENTS

13   The Parade

    *

15   Swim
16   3AM Porch Sitter
17   Thou
18   Closed I Know
19   Three Kinds of Singing
20   New Day
21   A Face
22   This Shocking Freedom and Its Violent and Sequined Consequences
23   Fear
24   The Fish
25   Awareness stares out

    *

27   The First Exhalation In A Long While Comes
28   The Conversation Below
29   A Dialectic
30   Jam Without Bread
31   Red Left The Painting
32   On Holiday, On The Plane
33   You Write the Poem
34   The peace you are waiting for

35	Who Did Time Belong To?
36	The Variations
37	The Spontaneous Poetry Booth (The Day I Was Keith Haring)
38	Criss-Cross
39	Shock
40	No Poem
41	Burns
42	About Now
43	Opening Your Email After A Long Absence

*

45	Do You Miss Your Old Life?
46	No Conversation
47	Grief Without Fantasy
48	Horoscope
49	Birthday Cake
50	Preserves
51	A Human Hug
52	The Vicks VapoRub of Poetry
53	Use These Poems
54	Bracelets Made of Scrabble Tiles
55	Translations in the Dark, or Last Night at the Artists' Colony
57	Someone looks at the menu
58	Song to the Specialty Channel with a Current Program, a Weather/Traffic Sidebar and Scrolling Headlines

59 The Bedroom Ceiling
60 The Translators' Party

    *

63 Generations
64 Seven Seascapes (Photographs, Gelatin Prints)
65 You, The Painting
66 Against the Rules
72 Risk
73 Earthquakes
74 A Request
75 This is Our Time
76 Who is Here
77 Palimpsest, or The Laughing Girl
78 Truths
79 Baffled Masters
80 Right in Front of Her
81 It Doesn't Matter

    *

83 *Notes*
85 *Acknowledgements*

The search for Reality is the most dangerous of all
undertakings, for it destroys the world in which you live.
— Nisargadatta Maharaj

    *

I am too scared to eat pie.
— Raymond Carver

THE PARADE

Yesterday the parade came through
with the elephants and trucks and bulldozers,
the tears of stoics,
the train of dresses and naked torsos;
the twirling and the shy.
They came through here. You were there, you saw it.
You were awake, you even encouraged it!
And it came through, blowy and clear.
The horns were distinct and raised to mouths.
They were so ready to be heard, how could they not be?
And they were heard. No one missed them.
You invited it all through you during the day
and in the evening did it all again
with other people, all these strangers seeming
to know each other. You raised your arms
to a symphony, delighting and thanking,
and then — *what happened then?* — you went to bed
tired, so tired
as though herds had run through you
but without evidence, except for the feeling
of earth kicked up or pounded down or both.

SWIM

The threads of you
drift away
like ink secreted and dissolving

I can't hold them
and whatever octopus sent out this ink
is floating away too

I watch you go and what I say
goes too and I don't know
what, if anything, there is to keep

or whether all there is to do
is watch the ink colour the water
we're in

and just swim

3AM PORCH SITTER

Cool in my light housecoat. 14 degrees Celsius.
Bare feet. Breezes.
I thought, it is only mild
disappointment, really, not
anger or longing. Oh. I thought
of the people in that movie,
characters, I was going to say.
I thought of how no one person
went past at this hour of the dark,
but taxis (and then
a man came quietly). I thought
there was no particular experience
to have or long for, not even sleep
or love; there was nowhere
else to be or get. Whatever
was seeing this was
steady, already there
and would be, though
evanescent in the thoughts
of packing and tea and
taxis and men and feet.

THOU

I have never understood the phrase
trembling before god.

It suggests a relationship
I don't have;

though I do tremble most mornings at 3AM
with no information and no witnesses.

I love the train whistle in the morning
for that very reason.

Trees shake in the wind, ripe or not.
Sometimes they break and litter the hills. Fruitless.

If thou has fear,
thou has company.

If thou runs through me like a fire
thou bears my gait.

CLOSED I KNOW

Closed I know how to be |
           open
I
flap around

These are not the wings of flight
soaring, majesty, etc.,
the long distance prophet offered,
just wings beating in readiness against the inside
of my chest. Can you hear?

They want me to wake up every hour
of the night. If it's 3AM, it's the kidneys
said the Japanese doctor. When is the hour
of the skin, the liver, the lung?

THREE KINDS OF SINGING

1
Heart pounds. Am I having
a heart attack, a panic attack,
an operatic episode, a triumph?
                 Shut up and listen.
Someone is singing on the radio. Now there are two.
Now there are three and one of them is me, though
my mouth is closed and the score is inside.

2
I had simply been smiling
as the man spoke of his victory, his
pride evident. *Why are you*
               smiling?
I can feel your delight, I said.
You can feel me. He said. Absorbing
the language on my face.

3
Heart pounds, making itself known.
And the rest, rests.
No more stories to carry.
              Soon, I said,
there won't even be
any words left in this poetry.

NEW DAY

All my categories are falling off their bodies.
She is beautiful. Or I am. Or neither. Or both.

This looks good or bad.
Or neither. Both.

I can't make out anything,
except what I like the moment I like it.

I walk around in new jeans
garmentless.

A FACE

Someone calls my name
and I become one of my smaller selves
so quickly winnowed.
Suddenly there is a face
where there was none
and it is one of mine.

Picture the illustration on the card of the illustrator:
bobble-shaped heads rolling, like carved pumpkins on a table.
In response, he'd said, to a poem about the faces we wear
for others. I had dismissed it then thinking I was above all that
and only wore one. Now I see
even one is too many

THIS SHOCKING FREEDOM AND ITS VIOLENT AND SEQUINED CONSEQUENCES

After the note that said I'd cut out your heart,
I didn't know if you were right and I was wrong. And how
clear I'd been, and how confused now, and how is it possible to
   be so baffled?

I saw then, no one to defend. No one to be absolutely right
ever. Because claw-toothed rage changes to phlegm
and back to teeth, there is no consistent self to be.

Which is why I could accurately be described a stranger
by you who loved me for years
because I was.

FEAR

Woke up today trembling.
One door open wider
than another door can handle.

THE FISH

I whisper to my friend *I have taken up meditation.*
I say it, allowing out of my mouth something foreign.
It lands on the table between us, blandly, like a plain fish;
as though I've said some innocent, salt-less thing
no one is much interested in.

I broke up with my lover
for this lover and now write poems about it.
That's why I whisper it across the table to my friend,
the very good poet, who looks at me with nothing in her face
I can read and says,

it doesn't matter what they're about, only
that they're good poems. She's right.
Everything is only itself. And needs to be
what it is. And then she leans over
and cuts perfectly into the poem.

AWARENESS STARES OUT

of the baby's eyes
nothing holds it together
it flies all over the room
shines on the wall
on paintings of gaudy-coloured gods.

It is a crow of light
reaching its one-toothed smile
across the room, then disappearing
into its crowing.

The crowing gets so loud
you can hardly bear this much awareness.

Now sharp-eyed darting again and then
the baby hides, lies down
in the absolute lap
of your awareness,
and sleeps.

THE FIRST EXHALATION IN A LONG WHILE COMES

The first exhalation in a long while comes
chased by goats. A staccato movement
on a hill. It is observed by
a shepherd, a dog, an old man and
woman holding hands, some sheep
and their dung. Enough
presence for a nice inhalation,
even a rest. Till the bleating
of the heart starts up again
requiring all these attendants
who are really just happening by
not doing much but, being
in the same place, enough.
It takes so little really to suspend breaking
with oneself, to stop stopping, to stay,
and it takes everything.

THE CONVERSATION BELOW

Sometimes I don't know what I am reading
but know the words have been put together like a secret puzzle
that reveals itself in my body,
so that tears come, bidden from some ancient
or childhood land with minarets and camels.

What do they know?
These fat tears on their swaybacks, dreamlike,
stepping forth, becoming real. Evidence
of the conversation

below the conversation, below silence, the one
I didn't know was carrying on
until the poets with their puzzles
like radio signal decoders
broke in.

A DIALECTIC

There is a dialectic happening
between the already free

and the caught
trying to get free.

It is happening in the wings.

flap flap
flap flap

JAM WITHOUT BREAD

1

Once I was at Sally's and it was Passover and I wasn't eating bread. And Sally, ever respectful said, Have some jam. It was tea time and there was Mary's treacle bread and Sally's cherry cake that looked a cake picture with only ever one slice removed and all kinds of half open jars of jam and wads of old cheese with the mould cut out and she said, Why don't you have some jam?

I said, It's Passover and I don't eat bread. I thought maybe she forgot. She said, Why don't you have some jam then, without bread? Why not? she said. It's only sugar and fruit.

2

Well, blow me down. I drive all the way to Stratford wanting Tim Horton's tea. 'But Balzac's!!' I hear myself say, 'Balzac's. The coffee's so good. You always go to Balzac's!!' So I go in and it smells dark-roasted, there are chairs empty and I look at the choices, think, *I even have a free one coming.* Buy a biscotti

go across the road where the white man round belly T-shirt dirty pants, daughter and greasy-haired woman are standing in front of me buying doughnuts. The woman says "there'll be fighting if I don't get the vanilla cream." They're loud, threaten not to take each other home and I know it's where I want to be. The words white trash I've been avoiding. Two old ladies, one with a hairnet, talk about cooking with potato chips.

I don't know why. The tea isn't even that good. But it's what I wanted. All the ideas of want — chai at Annapurna, croissants at Ezra's Pound, Balzac's — bypassed. Drove straight here in the downpour that fell overhead like a tunnel. When I've really advanced, I'll walk straight into what I want, even if it defies my mind, even if it surprises me.

RED LEFT THE PAINTING

Red left my eyes
in the highest heels.
I do and don't want people
to know, the red was mine,
I was crying.
I am so happy I can hardly
contain it, so it rises
off me in red smoke and red sounds.

ON HOLIDAY, ON THE PLANE

One day I went on holiday
and couldn't remember
any of my PIN numbers or passwords.
Stood at the payphone with nothing
coming out of my mind or fingers.

My teacher once said, *Let go of everything, just for this minute.*
Was that moment a taste?

And what if it went further and I forgot how to read?
If words meant nothing on the page; letters
went in nowhere; if they began
to float in all directions,
apart, like stars. Like no gravity

the way it is in the atmosphere where I am right now
if I just opened the door of the plane where I'm sitting
and stepped outside

YOU WRITE THE POEM

You write the poem
for such a simple reason
it's almost embarrassing —
in the moment of writing,
you don't care about anyone.

You take your shoes and socks off
in the middle of the painting.
You have no idea.
You disrobe like a hardboiled egg,
unshell.

The membranes built for years into
castles simply orgasm.
An old king
farts on his throne
and disappears.

THE PEACE YOU ARE WAITING FOR

will not come.   The sleep
you are wanting.   The space you are
longing to protect.

The body
you are trying to deplete and pump at the same time
will not do both.

There is nothing that will happen later.
There is no point saving it.

Time off isn't
about moments preserved.

It is not going to get quieter
until it is over
for good.

What are you going to do about it?   No one knows
what you are carrying nor will you get any points
for carrying it.

No one is waiting in the wings to ask
if they can hold you while you rest.

WHO DID TIME BELONG TO?

Time broke open like a shell
and all the old expectations
fell out in a floss and a jumble
in a yolk and a yoke and the yoke
broke.
The day looked empty or was
turned inside out like the lining
of a coat that disappeared when it reversed,
and there were no pockets of time
to hold anything in.
They disappeared or
I went into them
like air pockets.
And what that popping noise was
could not be identified.

THE VARIATIONS

You are in the world and I'm glad. And your friends are in the world. And this cellist is in the world with his boppy head and the woman in the red dress he nods to, who plays the violin beside him. They are in the world just below me, in a room surrounded by lunchtime people, this man from Chicago who said "you smell good," and I said "that's the best thing I've heard all day," these windows that go all the way up and all the way down to University in the rain, and an ambulance turning left, going north, though not in a hurry. And the buds in the courtyard are in the world, and the violist with his shiny shoes. Bach is in the world (*Bach is in the world!*) and the Goldberg Variations and my heart, and the streetcar going by on Queen Street, and the eyebrows of the cellist, and all their bows swinging across all their strings, and their ballet hands, and all the robin-breasted variations lifting off and lifting off and lifting off and lifting off at a lunchtime concert at noon.

THE SPONTANEOUS POETRY BOOTH
(THE DAY I WAS KEITH HARING)

I went with whatever their whim or wish
what the look on their face dictated —
reddening with self-consciousness,
stoic and pale. Stayed
with whoever was standing
in front of me. Wrote the poem
they wanted for a dollar. Anyone
in my periphery could not come into focus.
I was stunned dumb by questions, as though
some other Ronna took care of that
and I was only the janitor
here to clean up
the stormed heart, sweep it out,
assemble the dusty detritus, the dog-
mice of the mind, and put them
on a page and hope
for a filament that would alight
in the mind of the person opposite,
the mind of the room
      as it seemed to become
            the poem
                   trailing out after them
like a gown

CRISS-CROSS

All afternoon lines criss-cross my mind like trains that don't pause but keep
on moving in their tracks. Oh, I hear them!
As outside I hear all afternoon the wheels of an old
grocery cart rolling over the melting ice carrying
empties an old woman stacks for the liquor store twenty cents each.
No that's not what it is. It's the big wheel of a Big Wheeler
a boy rides up and down the sidewalk in his spring thrill. Could be.
But I've not gotten up from this bed most of the afternoon
and only participate in the day because my heart is pounding and my lungs
are tired on the shore, like collapsed dinghies or oil-soaked birds.
Breathing is hard today and lying down's better.
And after a dream of my teacher behind me, at a barbershop,
laughing and leaning forward to pat my knee, I am

refreshed. My brain shouts — you are fine! Go out! It is a beautiful
day! There is sun! Hurry, the cold is scheduled to return
with sundown. Hurry
the children are out, the old ladies with the rolling carriages,
everyone is moving and my heart
lifts a little
the lungs flap their wings
and the trains criss-cross my mind full of their cargo
of words some of which even reach
the air, but most
keep cruising off into the melting

SHOCK

These houses and restaurants
are now riddled with their gone owners,
the buildings like empties, the contents
drunk. I pass them thinking of those wines,
real bottles, and how we never drank them
together. Neighbours and shopkeepers standing
on uneven planes of connection. We pass
each other our little motes of wisdom
with Christmas cards and small tips.
We know each other only by first name, routine, shape
of a body from a distance, that intimacy. Our bare
glances — some days sour, some days soft —
our momentary poetries of exchange.
We disappear behind curtained windows,
or papered windows, or broken windows,
and into ambulances.
When we die
we don't come back.

NO POEM

There is no poem to hold the width,
the breadth, the depth, the time,
the words, the sounds, the colours.
No poem
to catch the light, the heat,
the radiator noises. There is
no poem for what we did,
or where we went, and how we
got here; and now,
no poem
to let us go.

BURNS

Write nothing today.
Allow it to grow inside you
until it bursts.
Marks on the page
and on your face like tiny burns,
apostrophes, cedillas, musical notes.
They come from inside and outside.
What is the word for that scorching?
It's raining and the sun
isn't visible.
But you know it's there.

ABOUT NOW

This longing, loneliness and sadness
are not about now.
How could they be?

The air smells sweet after the heavy
rain and the sky is bluing up again
with watercolour strokes of cloud

as the bulb comes on
by the beer billboard,
positioned in the centre of a live

matrix of wires and the brushstrokes
of cloud are going pink.
How could they?

OPENING YOUR EMAIL AFTER A LONG ABSENCE

And all those going conversations get loaded into your body like arrows, or like a thousand voice motet.

To survive is not to answer,
but to be pierced by sound.

*

DO YOU MISS YOUR OLD LIFE?

Now that I'm far from home
but not as far as he was
when he came over here last year,
I think of him, because of this distance.
Me from my home, him from his.
How he came to reflect on the trouble,
the two women he loved,
how we talked and talked, him cooking lamb
till the onions were soft but not stressed,
us drinking wine
and I asked all kinds of
questions I thought would help
or offer direction towards one shore or another,
and how now I only want to ask 'do you miss
your old life
now that you've waded so far out?'

That's where he was.

And when he was
heading back overseas to where
he now lives alone on a hill,
he showed me the gifts
for his kids,
and this notebook for his wife, this teapot
for his girlfriend. It was all factual like that
in separate white shopping bags.
Him going home to what he was
going home to, me the first time away
since I called it quits with my old life
and I'm asking myself
the same question —
without which
I'd really be at sea.

NO CONVERSATION

In my room again
doors shut for three days.

The delight of no conversation
makes me wonder how filled I've been
with conversation I don't want.

Forty-nine years is my whole history
of conversation.

The relief so vast
something opens

like a door in the wardrobe
of one of those stories I never read

because who had room
for imagination back then

when every nook was filled
with actual people
and their worries and requests?

It is so rich here in the unoccupied,
even boredom and loneliness
are precious.

GRIEF WITHOUT FANTASY

What I lost
was not going to happen.

I had
what happened.

There was no more.

HOROSCOPE

Your love life will be flat.
You may even be lonely.

Look ahead
the horizon is beautiful.

BIRTHDAY CAKE

In the vegetarian restaurant
the old woman's birthday cake is shared.
"No dairy! No dairy!" she calls.

Oily slices fall open
in pale layers
untouched. Poor cake. Divided and ignored.

Patrons eat
spinach curry instead, drink spiced tea, and the room
has so much noise. I read the poem

sent by a psychic poet in the east end, vexed.
This is not my poem. A mistake has been made on another plane.
Later, an alternate configuration of cells wakes up, remembers

great art; loves that were never mine, or were
so far back they were another person. Memory is stoked. So many layers.
Look at my plate.

Poor cake. In another life
you were *Schwarzvald, Sacher Torte*.
Mozart played when you came to the table.

People got up and danced.

PRESERVES

Today I found an intact jar of plum jam at the back
of the cupboard, it opened with a satisfying suck
and plummy smell. I made that jam, had

lost track. Was probably saving it.
Stop saving everything! Julia Child cries
touching my cheek.

Poetry opens me and I'm grateful. Thank God
for Grace Paley. She writes with her heart
and peasant body. And Adrienne Rich with that brow.

Is it just the High Holidays or my age?
I feel both more
and less Jewish around them.

Spend everything! they say. Here, have a plum.
The old women of culture come back, feed us,
tell us where we came from.

A HUMAN HUG

The day opens out
and the one I want is not in it;
but the birds with their cheap
trills and Susan Sontag hairdos
keep calling to each other
over the airwaves.
It's only 8 in the morning
but we've all been up since 4.
It's summer, the light
wants company
and the birds oblige.
One of them keeps repeating
the same name over again.
I understood it in my sleep,
but now that I'm awake,
it's only gibberish, bird language.

Every hour, a three-line poem repeated itself
like a snooze button going off in my head. It said
> I wanted a human
> hug, but realized I was already pressed up
> against the world.

It's true.
But it doesn't help
entirely. There's still
this body. The soul's tongue
can only taste so much.
Something screams for form.
Why else would we all be here
at this hour?

THE VICKS VAPORUB OF POETRY

I open the loving book
and put it face down on my heart.
The words go in.
A compassion lick.
Camphor, menthol, eucalyptus.

USE THESE POEMS

Use these poems as breaks in meetings that become tense
and threaten. Use them to alter
the wind in the room, the sail in the boat can fill
and go a different direction. Use them to stop the action
at customs, but be prepared to be detained
by Officer Deare. Resist calling him *dear*.
Use these poems as crutches for your eyes, splints
for the invisible bones.
Adrienne Rich says, Tonight no poetry will serve.
In the wider world, who has heard her voice.
Or fallen in love with a will that was understanding
and ferocious. Yoko Ono was not for everyone.
Use these poems to keep you warm any way you can. Burn them.
Their smoke won't smell of incense. But they will go up
and you will forget.
Memory isn't necessary.

It is late summer and the grief is in the field. If the husks
come off these poems and there's nothing there,
where will we go for food? All I really wanted
was to eat a little, rest, move my body,
love with and without fear, and lie down after work.
Hafiz says, Here's a pillow of words for comfort.
Take it, if it works, use these poems. Or leave them
on a plane, in someone else's bed, in an envelope
on the table, across the sentient grid.

BRACELETS MADE OF SCRABBLE TILES

I was given one word
around my wrist and it was
Symphony.
I needed nothing else
in a bracelet made of scrabble tiles.

I felt all the knots inside untie
like ribbons,
and I gave them
to the tomato plants
so they could stand up straight.

And the knotted wood
he kept in the garage
too good
to throw out
was made into his coffin.

Perhaps there is a use
for everything.
Though the cynic rears up and says
Wars? Genocides? Suicides?
And I have no answer.

TRANSLATIONS IN THE DARK, OR
LAST NIGHT AT THE ARTISTS' COLONY

1
Something began to disintegrate,
atmospheric, atomic and particular. Hail stones
of yesterday's pre-blackout, the integers
of the internet clogged with the passing traffic
streaming to get through while the town was down
and dark but still selling liquor from basements
one bottle at a time if you had exact change.
We drank in the dark wearing miners' lights
to read our poems. It was only words
but we traded them and they would
go home to our respective
countries on different planes within days.
Moving into our bodies through drink, muscle ring,
laughter, pores; texting by moonlight and
undiluted this morning; the lines still full;
my back wanted a physical
equivalent, someone to hold, their arms around my back.
I couldn't be the only one needing this kind
of carnal solution; no wonder there's so much
rampant sex in these camps. It's not just the flinging
of boundaries, but the positive dissolution, the self-stripped soul
releasing.

2
Someone called this an asylum for the sane.
If that's the case, a more radical translation
will be necessary to take this madness
home. It will be less work
if we speak in the language of the shiva house:
that community of ecstatic grief, of doors
that stay open all night and we stream through;
and when there's nothing more to say
thump our chests in greeting and wait for the moment

in the evening when it's time
to sing, which we do by heart, letting
our minds continue
to slide out from under us.

SOMEONE LOOKS AT THE MENU

says to her friend
what do you feel like? And it fills you with longing
for the one who says: would you like a delicious
chicken sandwich, dear? for the one who says
would you like to take a bath in the afternoon?
I have towels. Have a rest. For the one who
says, go, make the call, I'll be right here, watching.
For the one who says *I have faith in you*
does not stand apart. Or stands apart but
does not leave you.

SONG TO THE SPECIALTY CHANNEL WITH A CURRENT PROGRAM, A WEATHER/TRAFFIC SIDEBAR AND SCROLLING HEADLINES

Oh, poor you, you're so busy.
How do you keep track of yourself?
Is it that you've let yourself go?

Your words fly across the bottom of your body
and your wind chills are high. What do you need?
Cloudy with a fire in the basement.
Is there anything I can offer?

THE BEDROOM CEILING

When I first moved in I hated it
with such a vengeance it made
me angry and ashamed.
Now I can't remember why.
I have seen so many faces in the raised
plaster moons, the swirls of white
icing. I even saw Faye Dunaway once
a few years back, when my husband still lay
beside me. But she was
much younger then. Now when I look up
my eyes blur and clear
like a throat about to speak.

THE TRANSLATORS' PARTY

The man who read Heraclitus, first in Greek,
then in English in his own oracular voice.
The Hungarian with Rapunzel grey hair.
The Greek man with the white scarf
born in Drama.
The woman turning Metis into Catalan.
Hungarian and French
side by side carry on their tongues a man in a coma,
one begins to cry, a waving away of the hand.
The Dutch man in Dada, standing on the table
singing of a Singer sewing machine
through a bottomless paper-cup megaphone, spinning
so the whole room can hear him.
The Greek woman with the hair. The man
doing Brooklyn. The Quebecois' apology
to those who don't understand, his souvenir.
The woman from Serbia, the one from Santiago de Cuba,
California. Everyone in their language and then in
someone else's, drinking wine, standing up, sitting down,
one after another, blurring,
not becoming one.

*

GENERATIONS

When they blew, all the silos emptied
into the same land.
All the sadness was the same sadness

and we stood there
in the red field or the purple field
in surprise.

SEVEN SEASCAPES
(PHOTOGRAPHS, GELATIN PRINTS)

There were seven seas
and they were different seas.

This one forebode, turning darkly.
This one teemed with light.

The third sea from the right
steamed like Rothko. Stretches

of air, water.
A light in the centre getting smaller

dimming as the ripples showed up.
The Aegean said: no you can't.

The word 'print' was a lie.
Nothing could be that solid,

but the density of the dark
stomach.

There were seven seas and they were different
but they were all ocean.

YOU, THE PAINTING

Every heart stood in front of you, as in front of a painting, and looked, and you could feel them looking

emanating, choral —

    absolutely silent, absolutely sound.

AGAINST THE RULES

1
She was a ballet dancer
she was a sugar cube
rolling on the floor and melting.
Or she might have been. But she stood beside herself
in self consciousness watching the piano player's hands
rolling. Turns out sweetness couldn't be stopped
it rolled on inside her
though she didn't know it,
kept moving in order not to know.
When it got touched, she'd open
the way a mollusc opens, and then she would close,

she'd get into her car and drive before sunrise
no goodbyes, not noticing the closing
until another might notice, and when they'd ask why,
why would stick a stick in her, a prod, a recognition
and then a further closure; a highway strewn with bags,
pieces of tire coming off trucks she'd swerve
to miss. Driving was god
she was fast and the gearshifts
ground down; she pushed through
three countries, drove across worlds
until one person noticed, said
you've been on the road a third of your life.

Where was she going?
How far would a person travel
to meet and escape their heart?
There was no next: moving
was a kind of cutting
an unfurling
a holy book
a holy book she didn't want, that

tasted bad, that smelled of old men
and ass; tucked away in someone else's pleasure
and disgusting to her. The book would not come out of her
this book would not
come into her, though
it was there in the notes, the music
already rolling, laid down
in the body where it belonged.

2

I have written this before: the girl was
diminished; she was wasted; she was
waiting. She was comfortable
in grief, loss easier than losing. I have confided this
and I'm afraid of losing you, of your eyes
glazing. You know this story: it's every girl's story.
This part for you. (This part for me.)
A long division, a cellular division,
invisible. The perfecting
of public vulnerability
and the mollusc of the holy book. Shelled.
Shell-shocked. Never mind.
You're not interested.

3

She travelled to holy places. Ireland, Israel.
She dipped her toes in and opened, in places
where she was strange.
Everyone who is a mollusc knows that
travel is the safety of the soul. Or its suitcase.
The perpetually new. But even the new
develops its patterns. Loves lock
down. The morning café that is
welcome becomes worn,
the men who stand at the bar or sit
in the back with their books, the women
who flow in in small knots of legs and smiles;

the server who knows her order knows
her order though she is never known.
Never known to herself as she never
opens the book of herself. Whose
book is it?

She travelled to places where
holy books were revered, stuffed
into walls. She went to Wales,
to a tiny town with thirteen bookstores, one
open all night where you drop
the money into a locked box. The books
were strewn on the floor,
a sacrilege she sat in.

She could not read; the words
dissolved into sleep with the light
left on. She turned away: once
a place of comfort, a bookstore where her bowels
would relax became a sea-blur of shelves. How
could anyone choose? A schizophrenic
held a camera once and did not know what to shoot.
She was an open shutter.
But she was a closed shutter.

4
Are you waiting for the story of transformation,
the bleeding, the stone, the eagle that cracked
her open? I will not give it.
You must love the closed.

5
She went to places where the book of herself
could be opened. But she couldn't
read. How could she read the book of herself
which included things she'd seen and felt
and knew and sung and danced, and hated and
feared and stifled and cradled?

In the trees, in the fog, in the mountains,
in cafés, in other languages, with or without
sirens, with or without snow. She walked
like the opening scene of a film she once saw:
a man walking straight out of his life.
                              She walked.
Wore her fear as armour;
as scapula; as adornment.
She was fiercely curtained,
the sweetness rolling below.
But anyone could see what she was.
Everyone sees everything.

6

The abuse was not sexual.
(Though there was that.)
It was theological.
There was the rape
of the eyes. When you are
open, everything gets in

7

and in that open nothing to hide: saliva
in the corners of their mouths. Kaleidoscope
of teachers who loved her the way they did.
The atmosphere and texture. The infrared of invasion.
Who wouldn't keep the book of themselves locked?
Who could trust even to their own knowing?
In the spiritual fuck and the sexually corrupt surround:
the kaleidoscope of naked bodies, of dumped bone
with nothing but facts to clothe them, the kaleidoscope
goes in through the same eyes that see
the five books of holy, 613 laws, and if a cow
falls on your land what are your remedies
and if someone takes your land what are your
remedies and if you are carted off in a train
what are your remedies and if you say the name of

god, the name of god or God,
rather than spell it, what will be your remedy
and who will mete it?
Who will harden their heart against you?

And the Lord hardened his heart to his people.

8
She hardened her heart. She learnt.
The body has its way of knowing.
Though only the wilfully sightless bought it.
Anyone looking could see what she was.
She thought no one could, but they saw everything:
the exterior suitcase and the inner soft. And when they saw,
    she moved,
kept moving
until the houses between moves became pauses and no one could
    keep going
that long that hard that tired that thin that scared
that hopeless.

9
In those days, in that place, for that girl:
incursion, fear. The great teachers
of the school followed her home,
followed her on her walk the 613 blocks
from one to the other and back. A community
of fear. Forbidden. On certain days. Unclean.
At certain times. Until even hello was a danger
and the route and the lawmakers between.

10
And yet she loved the book.

11
The book was a piece of land with two titles, a cow
with two owners, a baby taken into a king's
loving hands. One could tear it apart or give it back.

And I will tell you what happened.
Although and because it is against the rules
I will tell you.

There is no — .

And when this that is true rolled and stopped at her feet
she could open it.

This truth that could roll and roll like a sugar cube
across worlds, melting.

Anyone looking could see that she was gone.
Anyone looking could see that:
the traveller who drove before sunrise…

RISK

You carried your heart
like a bowl of light.
Nobody knew. Though some
looked in your direction,
askance.
So what.
That didn't stop you.
People often stop being themselves
because of the bad press,
and when they have to.
Some act in secret. Lovers
offer what they dare,
the possibility of massacres
all around them.

EARTHQUAKES

   For *relief* I gave $2 at the grocery store.
"Which relief?" I asked the matter-of-fact cashier.
"The Asian one," she said, sending her finger back
   over her shoulder, motioning in the direction
   of last week. My head swirled
   with disaster. Hurricane, Cyclone, Famine, AIDS.
Does it matter? I thought
   and looked at the girl's face that broke nothing.
Around the world people gathered.
Send it somewhere. Put it in a pocket.

A REQUEST

Look at their eyes. Go as far
in as the twitching, flaming
worry-fringe of their eyebrows, as far
as the exchange of rods and cones,
the crystal-blue iris, the black on black,
the mulish brown. Go as far back
as their motherlands. As far
as they will let you
and then,
make a space for respect, a breathing
distance for them to come
                    forward.

THIS IS OUR TIME

The words arrive to say: this is it. There is no other
time for us. And also
there was a time that wasn't ours. Also:
there will be. And it is moving quickly.

Something made me think of Sam.
How big he was in my world
now gone.
How a hundred years ago
there was an equally big
Sam who had a whole world
of people love and struggle with him.
And coming up,
there'll be another I won't know.

But it's possible that right now
I'm Sam.
We are.

WHO IS HERE

Beethoven
Rilke
Rumi
and Hafiz.
Wikipedia

telling their dates deaths deafnesses
rages rants passions and codas, movements
sforzando sforzando
isolation love desolation love.
12th, 16th, 18th, 19th century.

Here in this round room
in the trees in the mountains
in the rain in the sun, no one
no one no one no one.

PALIMPSEST, OR THE LAUGHING GIRL

The laughing girl looks a lot like me
and I don't know what she's laughing at.
She is in my head like a clip from a film.
Why is she laughing when I only ever
picture her miserable and alone.
What's so funny? But she just
continues to laugh, facing
left. Maybe she isn't
me at all. Who then?
Stop it or get out.
She refuses to stop. Churlish.
Not a word I'd use
on my childhood self, one whose smile
was only half a mouth wide, not
this big laughter taking up residence and claiming
to be me.
Oh, I'm getting another movie here.
One underneath the one that I remember.
One that would have frothed to the surface
had it not sunk down from ridicule
and just this sort of interrogation.
Now she is laughing and won't tell me why.
"Get used to it," she says,
and throws back her head.

TRUTHS

> I don't like what happened to my sister.
> — LEONARD COHEN

I am a big crier.
And angry. For what
happened.

And what I didn't know.
And what I know now.
And what I might never know.

BAFFLED MASTERS

1
The toddlers in the ravine are obedient
except for Toby. Hear the teacher scold *Toby,
you are being silly Toby* while everyone else
holds the rope that joins them like tiny
mountain climbers.

2
A woman in a Tuscan boutique
wearing stilettos and a tight skirt, severe and dark
with fierce lips, went to a cupboard in the back,
did a frantic dance, a little mad jig to no music
but that ringing in her head, came out again and resumed her face.

3
Within inches of each other the signs:
you are leaving the off-leash area
you are entering the off-leash area.
The poor dogs and their baffled masters don't know
whether to be released, and where.

RIGHT IN FRONT OF HER

She had been sitting in that room
all her life, waiting
for him to notice her.
She was waiting
for him to say it was ok.
She was waiting for him
not to need her
to wait; and she'd be waiting there
still

if he hadn't dissolved right in front of her
when she suddenly noticed
how he'd never noticed;
and how it could go on
no longer.
He was instantly
broken

and from his halves light clouded up
and she dropped her shoulders, the light
went into her and she went,
got up and left,
or left before getting up,
no one was there, no one waiting
for nothing,
and the room itself empty,
and then gone,
filled with no one
left waiting

IT DOESN'T MATTER

It really doesn't matter how long you loved.
Some insects only live for a day
and their love matters
though it's blind.
Your heart hurts literally
and all you can see
are mushroom clouds,
slow-motion photographs
of flowers opening
and a dry kernel
of corn in steam
just before it burns.

NOTES

The illustration on the card in "A Face" is by Jerry Silverberg.

"Shock" is in memory of Carlo Tela.

"The Vicks VapoRub of Poetry" came after reading a poem by Kabir. I can't remember which.

The bracelet in "Bracelets Made of Scrabble Tiles" was made by Liz Zetlin.

The translators in "The Translators' Party" and "Translations in the Dark" were participants in the Banff International Literary Translation Centre (BILTC) at The Banff Centre, 2011.

"Seven Seascapes, (Photographs, Gelatin Prints)" is a response to Hiroshi Sugimoto's 2007 exhibition at the Royal Ontario Museum, *History of History*.

"Against The Rules" was written with the felt influence of Shalom Auslander's memoir, *Foreskin's Lament* (Penguin Books, 2007).

ACKNOWLEDGEMENTS

I would like to thank the editors of the following journals and the anthology in which some of these poems appeared, sometimes in earlier versions or with different titles: *Grain, Our Times Magazine, The Shir Libeynu High Holiday Supplement, 2011, Draft 7.2, CRAVE IT: Writers and Artists Do Food* (Red Claw Press, 2010).

Thank you to The Banff Centre Leighton Artists' Colony, Annapurna Restaurant of Bathurst Street, Toronto, and the University of Toronto Poet in Community partners for residencies, hospitality and generosity during the writing of this book.

Thanks also to my excellent editor, publisher and ally, Beth Follett. She informed me that the word 'heart' appears thirteen times in this collection. Too many? Here are two more: I extend my heart of hearts in appreciation to the friends, family, teachers and students who laugh and cry with me. And to the stranger picking up this book. In gratitude.

RONNA BLOOM has published four previous books of poetry, most recently *Permiso* (Pedlar Press, 2009). Her poems have been broadcast on CBC, displayed on public hoardings (a Poetry Is Public initiative (www.poetryispublic.ca)) and recorded by the Canadian National Institute for the Blind. These days the ground shifts across her work as Poet in Community at the University of Toronto, a psychotherapy practice, a meditation practice, and writing and performing poetry. Whatever the focus, the aim is for the widest possible experience of receptivity and responsiveness, and in that sense it's all one thing. | www.ronnabloom.com